A Primer on Negotiating Corporate Purchase Contracts

A Primer on Negotiating Corporate Purchase Contracts

Patrick C. Penfield

A Primer on Negotiating Corporate Purchase Contracts

First published in 2010 by
Business Expert Press, LLC
222 East 46th Street, New York, NY 10017
www.businessexpertpress.com

ISBN-13: 978-1-60649-259-8 (paperback)
ISBN-13: 978-1-60649-096-9 (e-book)

DOI: 10.4128/9781606490969

Business Expert Press Supply and Operations Management Collection

Collection ISSN: 2156-8189 (print)
Collection ISSN: 2156-8200 (electronic)

Cover design by Jonathan Pennell
Interior design by Scribe, Inc.

First edition: March 2010

10 9 8 7 6 5 4 3 2 1

Printed in the United States of America.

Abstract

In today's world everyone is looking for cost reduction opportunities. The main opportunity to reduce costs is through negotiations with suppliers. Many companies struggle with the "methodology" in order to prepare for a negotiation. This book was written to help buyers develop a road map to negotiation success. Planning for a negotiation is an important skill set that can impact the bottom line and help your company save money. The process within this book has saved companies millions of dollars!

Keywords

Purchasing, negotiations, planning, cost savings, negotiation process, goals and objectives, suppliers, contracts, rebates, strategy, negotiation tactics, cost reductions, terms, discounts, planning, checklists, supplier selection, boilerplate, termination clauses

Contents

Acknowledgments

To my Mom, who taught me that anyone can succeed regardless of adversity. To Kristen, who believed in my efforts and inspired me to get this book published.

To Patrick and Julia for allowing me the time to write and research this book: I love you guys!

To my mother-in-law, Jane Sozzi, for all her help in editing this book (M.E.L.).

Introduction

In most companies, the purchasing department is called upon to improve quality, delivery, and service and to control or reduce costs on the parts, products, or services they purchase for their company. It is about getting the right thing at the right price at the right time to the right place. Purchasing's primary function is to negotiate the best possible deal. Many times, buyers will enter into a negotiation without any type of game plan. They will start the negotiation without any goals or objectives and usually are surprised at the outcome of the agreement. Negotiation is like a chess game: you need to have a game plan *before* you start.

The ultimate goal in chess is to checkmate your opponent's king. In a negotiation, the ultimate goal is to meet the objectives and goals you have developed. Before an experienced chess player starts a chess match, he or she develops a game plan for his or her opponent. Typically, a professional chess player will have a reputation and a methodology in playing the game. In a negotiation, you also need to develop a strategy for your supplier. Is the person you are negotiating with a skilled negotiator? Is he or she an experienced negotiator or new to negotiating? What type of negotiation strategy does the supplier employ? These are some of the questions that you should ask yourself before you go into a negotiation. Throughout this book I will provide a step-by-step guide on how to plan a negotiation.

CHAPTER 1

Planning

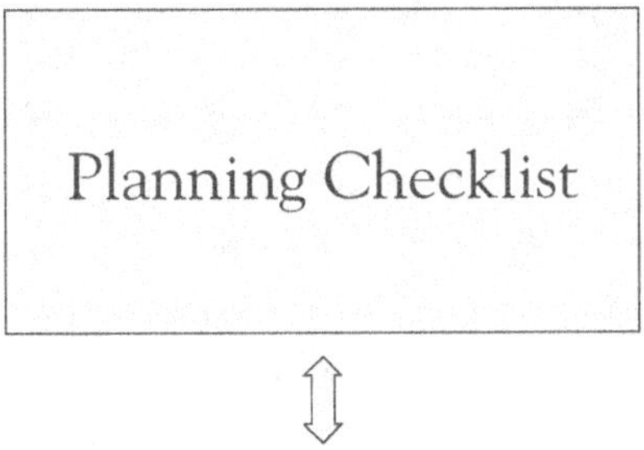

Planning Checklist

Figure 1.1.

Sadly, planning for negotiations has been largely forgotten in most purchasing departments. In the book *Managing Purchasing* by Killen and Kamauff, they state that "planning can be defined as a process of deciding in advance what is to be done, who is to do it, how and when it is to be done, and how well it is to be done."[1] Most of us are so busy with the day-to-day activities in our purchasing departments that we forget to properly plan for a negotiation. When I was attending college for my undergraduate degree, a friend of mine saw that I was frantically finishing up some schoolwork before the end of the semester break. He was sitting on a couch in our dorm room reading the paper. As I walked past him, he said, "Remember the rule of the five Ps." I asked him, what is the rule of the five Ps? He stated that the five Ps stands for "proper planning prevents poor performance." I laughed and commented, "You should have told me this at the beginning of the semester." It has been 18 years since this comment was made to me, but I still try to live by the five Ps.

All purchasing departments should have some type of business plan that they are trying to achieve. A business plan tells you what goals you are trying to reach as an organization and is typically written by the department head. The business plan is usually between 3 to 5 years and includes your department's mission statement, vision statement, and succession plan. It states your strategies on supplier reductions, supplier certification, technological advancements, and cost savings. The business plan drives your negotiation strategies. The objective is to meet your cost savings portion of the business plan. Once you have a business plan, you have an idea of where you need to be from a cost savings perspective. The problem with developing a plan can be the execution of the plan itself. Most of us are doing more work with less people. If we are too busy to properly plan for our negotiations, success may be compromised. Did you know that every dollar we save in purchasing goes straight to the bottom line on most profit and loss statements? Why do we have such a hard time preparing for a negotiation? Most of the time we have no format to use in planning our negotiations. How can we expect to be successful when we don't even know how to develop a game plan?

In professional football, a team will develop a game plan for the opponent they are playing that week. They will look at the weaknesses of the opposing team in the game plan. Once they have finished the analysis, they will develop a strategy to take advantage of those weaknesses. They will also incorporate what their strengths are in the game plan and develop special plays to take advantage of the other team's weaknesses. Each team will spend countless hours researching the other team. They will watch films on the opposing team from past games, research current injuries to team members, and practice executing the game plan for several days before they actually play the game. Each player on the team will understand his role in the game plan. How many of us actually prepare this much for a negotiation? Do we even know what information or structure we should use in preparing for a negotiation? We need to take the time to develop a game plan that will take advantage of our strengths and our opponent's weaknesses during a negotiation. This book will help you prepare a game plan so that you can win in your negotiations.

How long should a negotiation take? Allow yourself 4 months to start and finish the negotiation. Contracts are usually the roadblock in most negotiations. Legal departments like to debate every clause in a contract. Some contracts take years to be approved. Figure 1.2 is a flowchart showing a typical contract execution process.

Figure 1.3 is a planning checklist for your negotiation. I have added an example of a negotiation with a fastener company throughout the book. There is also a blank sheet you can use for future negotiations.

All of this information needs to be documented and kept in the supplier's file. When we document past negotiations, it helps us keep a history on that supplier, which we could potentially use in our next negotiation. The key items that should be included in the file are the checklists contained in this book. The checklist in Figure 1.3 will help you plan your negotiation.

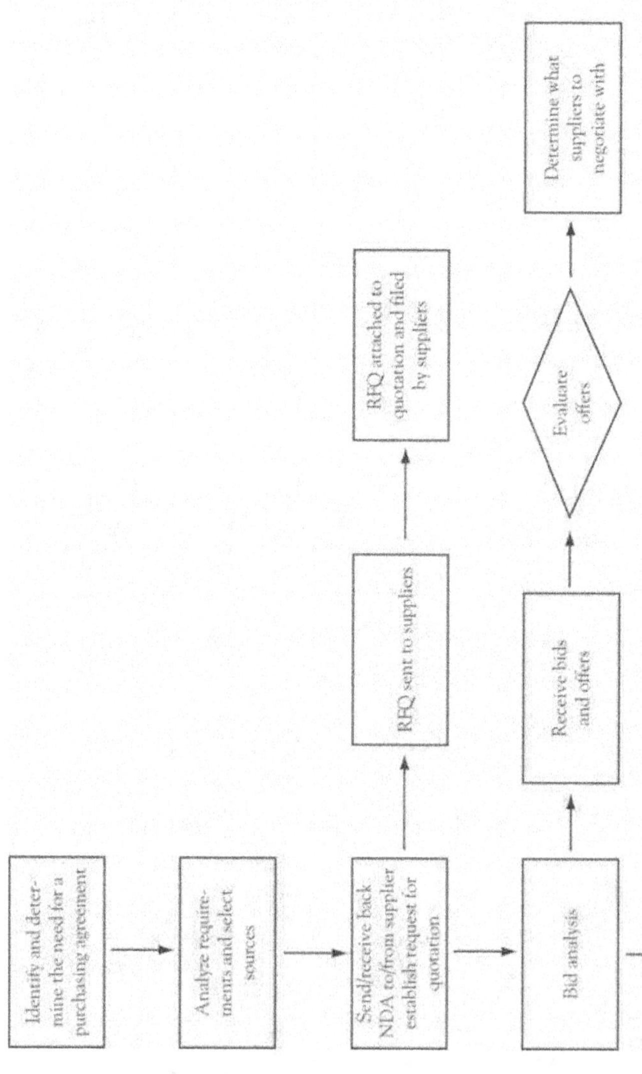

Identify and determine the need for a purchasing agreement
Analyze requirements and select sources
Send/receive back NDA to/from supplier establish request for quotation
Bid analysis
RFQ sent to suppliers
RFQ attached to quotation and filed by suppliers
Receive bids and offers
Evaluate offers
Determine what suppliers to negotiate with

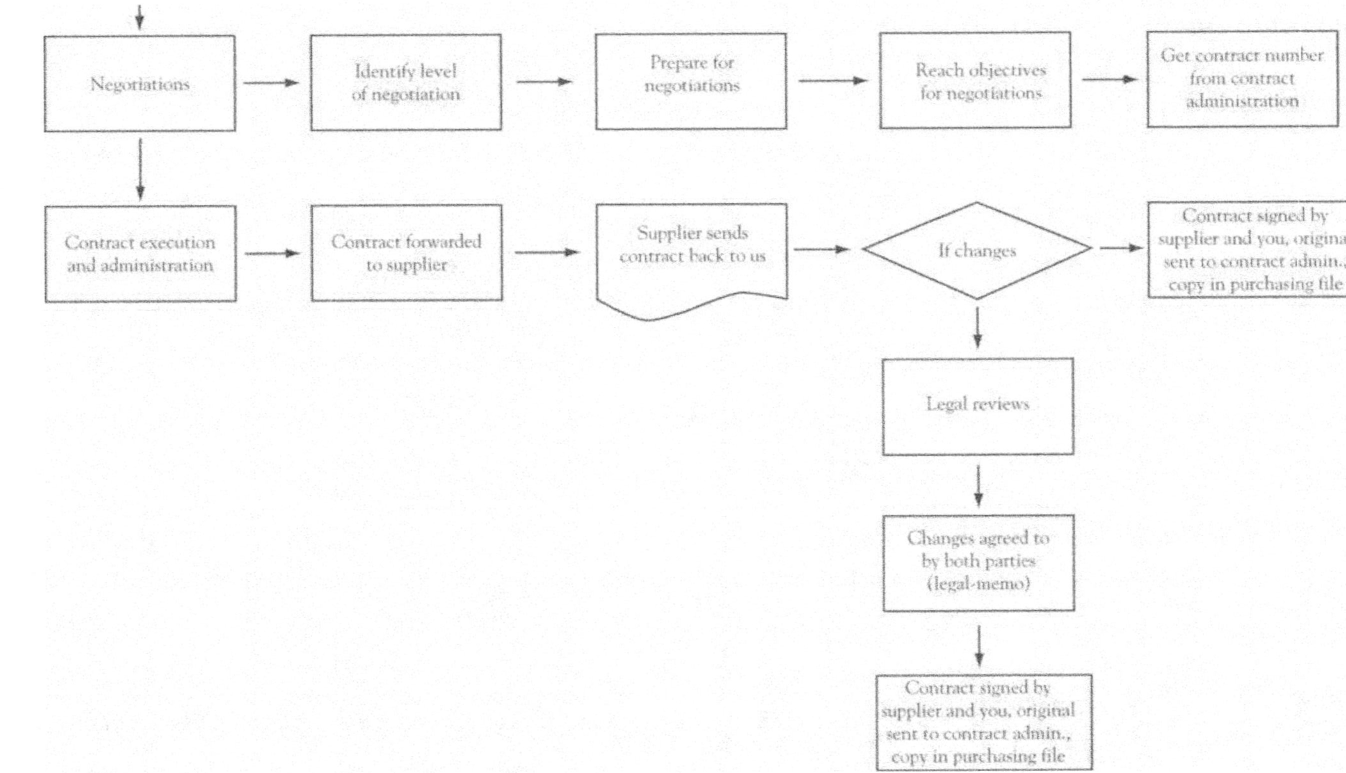

Figure 1.2. Contract execution flowchart

New Agreement

Agreement Number: <u>Fas – 01/20/00-1</u>

Proposed Contract Period

<u>4/15/2000</u> to <u>4/15/2003</u>

Commodity: <u>Fasteners</u>

Company Name: <u>Highway Fasteners Inc.</u>

Team:			**Division**
Lead Negotiator:	Joel Smith	of	Buffalo
Representative:	Agnes Mitt	of	Syracuse
Representative:		of	

Forecast:	**Dollar Value**	**Percentage**
Buffalo	$100,000	91%
Syracuse	$10,000	9%
Total	$110,000	100%

Comments:

Highway has been a supplier of ours for the past 10 years. They have recently opened a China operation to take advantage of lower costs. We are due for some major cost reductions.

Status:

Forecast Due: <u>1/15/00</u>   Negotiations: <u>3/22/00</u>

RFQ: <u>2/15/00</u>   Sign Contract: <u>4/01/00</u>

Bid Close: <u>3/15/00</u>   System Load: <u>4/15/00</u>

Bid Analysis: <u>3/22/00</u>

Results:	$ of Inc / Dec	% of Inc / Dec
Buffalo		
Other Division		

Benefits ____

New Agreement

Agreement Number: ________________________

Proposed Contract Period

________________ to ________________

Commodity: ____

Company Name: ____________________________________

Team:		**Division**
Lead Negotiator:	____________ of	____________
Representative:	____________ of	____________
Representative:	____________ of	____________

Forecast:	Dollar Value	Percentage
Other Division	____________	____________
Total	____________	____________

Comments:

____

____

Status:

Forecast Due: ________________	Negotiations: ________________
RFQ: ________________	Sign Contract: ________________
Bid Close: ________________	System Load: ________________
Bid Analysis: ________________	

Results:	$ of Inc / Dec	% of Inc / Dec
Other Division	____________	____________

Benefits ____

Figure 1.3. New agreement

CHAPTER 2

Supplier History and Intelligence

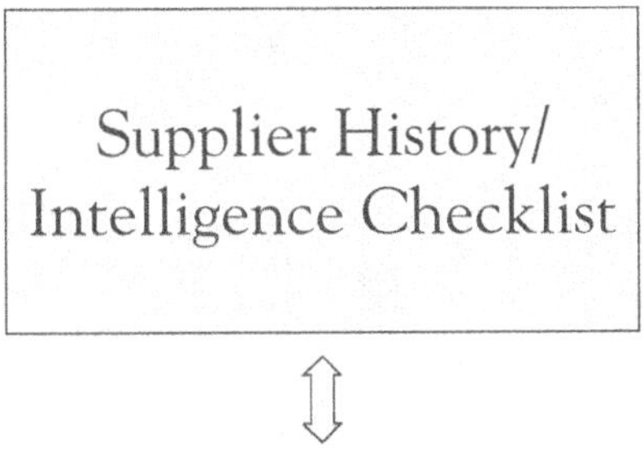

Supplier History/
Intelligence Checklist

Figure 2.1.

One of the first things that needs to occur before you begin your planning is to gather as much intelligence as you can on the supplier with whom you are negotiating. This information will help you plan your negotiation. What do I mean by intelligence? Intelligence is any information you can get on a supplier.

At the start of the negotiation you should seek out all the history you can on a supplier and the company. Next, you need to understand what is going on in the world today. What is going on with inflation, unemployment, and the financial markets? It is important to know which areas are booming and which are not.

We live in a global economy, and it is important to understand that what goes on in the world today may affect us. Next, find out all you can about the supplier's industry. In the book *The Road to Class A Manufacturing Resource Planning (MRP II)* by Tincher and Sheldon, they quote the Chinese philosopher and general Sun Tzu, who lived more than 2,500 years ago: "If you know the enemy and know yourself, you need not fear the result of a hundred battles. If you know yourself but not the enemy, for every victory gained you will also suffer a defeat. If you know neither the enemy nor yourself, you will succumb in every battle."[1] Although Sun Tzu was referring to war with weapon-toting enemies, these ideas seem to fit today's highly competitive market. You need to find out what is going on with the supplier's company, how they are doing financially, what investments they are making, who is their competition, and what are they planning for the future (research and development). Some of this information will be given to you by the supplier and the other information you will have to find. Ideally, you want to find out a company's profitability, gross margin, capacity utilization, debt, backlogs, delivery performance, and how large a customer you will be to this company. A friend of mine used to call the receptionist of a big supplier prior to a negotiation. Unknowingly, she would give him all the information he needed to develop a game plan.

The World Wide Web is probably the best place to get information on a supplier. Using any search engine (e.g., Google) should help you find plenty of information on that company. The *Wall Street Journal* is another excellent resource for information on a company. A supplier's local newspaper is another source you can tap into to find out what is going on with that company. Your public library will have information on your suppliers. Ask the librarian where you can get information on a supplier other than newspapers. Dun & Bradstreet (D&B) is an excellent source of financial information on a supplier. The D&B report will reveal the financial condition of your supplier by showing you how well your supplier pays bills and their credit worthiness. This is an important report that should be run before each negotiation. The next thing you need to do is to start generating commodity information on your supplier. Identify what the purchased parts are used in and on and what the commodity is for those parts (i.e., bearings, motors, etc.). Next, find out how long you have been purchasing parts from this supplier. Have you been buying parts from this supplier for over 5, 10, or 15 years? Find out what the price increases or decreases have been over the years you have been doing business.

A lot of companies fail to retain such history. This can cause a problem when a buyer leaves the company, taking all history on past negotiations with him or her. Hopefully, all of this is documented in your supplier files. It is beneficial to map out your cost increases or decreases, so you can compare what's going on in the world to your supplier's price adjustments. This will also give you an understanding of how well your supplier is controlling the costs. Your supplier should give you a breakdown of what other costs are associated with your product. What percentage of costs is made up by materials, labor, overhead, and profit margin? Many suppliers do not like to give out information on profit margin. All companies are in business to do one thing, and that is to make money. Suppliers have the right to make money on the parts they sell to you. You need them to be profitable and healthy.

If a supplier is unwilling to tell you how much profit he or she is making, you can usually find out through a book titled *Standard & Poor's Profit Margin by Industry* (also accessible online). This book will tell you your supplier's average profit margin per industry. The easiest way to see if your supplier is overcharging you on your product is to market test the parts you purchase from them. A market test sends a "request for quote" (RFQ) to several other suppliers to gauge if you are getting the best price on the market.

We live in a capital-driven society, where the fittest survive in regard to price and quality. It's important to make sure suppliers realize this. They have to be up to the challenge of decreasing their prices and constantly striving to improve the products they offer. If the results of your market test show that your current supplier's prices are out of line but they are a good supplier, you should give them the opportunity to match these prices. A supplier has to realize that competition is everywhere and that we are constantly striving to improve our operations. If the supplier does not want to match these prices, then you seriously have to consider doing business with other companies who can. This in itself can be a traumatic event, but we live in a changing world. As buyers, we should always be watching to see where technology is going. As one purchasing manager told me, we should work with our suppliers but always with an eye toward new technology or innovation that may help us overtake our competition. The society we live in is changing rapidly, and we all have to be at the forefront of change. Suppliers need to understand and realize this and embrace change and competition. What if your supplier is in a sole source situation? You cannot market test their products because there is nowhere else to go. There are situations where this will occur, but many companies these days are hungry for business, and almost every supplier has a competitor. Another problem at times is getting the engineering time to approve a new source. Many new suppliers will volunteer to pay for the engineering time to approve their parts. All we have to do is ask! All suppliers have to realize that eventually a company will take appropriate action when there is an abusive situation occurring. It surprises me that suppliers will sometimes "bite the hand that feeds them." Usually, in these situations, a supplier has become too big or arrogant and will not remain your supplier for too long. Figure 2.2 is a checklist to use when investigating a supplier.

Supplier Profile

Supplier   __Highway Fasteners Inc.__   Supplier Code   __0007__

Service:

What do you claim for shipping performance: __95%__

Average dollar value shipped each month: __$50,000__

Backorders are usually complete within: __3 days__

Other Information:

Date of Last Supplier Assessment: __1/99__   Rating: __100%__

Contract Expiration: __4/15/00__

Last Year's Performance Scoring: __95%__

Quality: __95%__   Delivery: __95%__   Service: __95%__

Union Affiliation: __None__

Total Number of Employees: __15__   Salaried: __4__   Hourly: __11__

Financial:

Annual Sales Volume: __$600,000__   Rated by DB: __Good__

DB Number: __1678-96-3__ Is there a Financial Statement Available? __Yes – See Attached__

Planned expansion / capital expenditures: __Yes – expanding 20,000 square feet__

** Please attach current Dun and Bradstreet report. **

Quality:

Are you ISO Certified? __Yes__   Are you QS 9000? __Yes__

Are you utilizing SPC? __Yes__   Do you have a quality manual? __Yes__

Warranty Return Information

Who is the company contact for warranty returns: __Joe Cool__

Address: __1700 Highway Lane__

City: __Buffalo__   State: __New York__   Zip: __13027__

Phone: __716-824-3003__   Fax: __716-824-5120__

Parent Company Name: __None__

Address: ______________________________

City: __________   State: __________   Zip: __________

Phone: __________   Fax: __________

Supplier Profile

Supplier ____________ Supplier Code ______________

Service:

What do you claim for shipping performance: _________________________________

Average dollar value shipped each month: _________________________________

Backorders are usually complete within: _________________________________

Other Information: _________________________________

Date of Last Supplier Assessment: __________ Rating: __________

Contract Expiration: _________________________________

Last Year's Performance Scoring: _________________________________

           Quality: __________ Delivery: __________ Service: __________

Union Affiliation: _________________________________

Total Number of Employees: ____________ Salaried: __________ Hourly: __________

Financial:

Annual Sales Volume: __________ Rated by DB: _________________________

DB Number: _______________ Is there a Financial Statement Available? ____________

Planned expansion / capital expenditures: _________________________________

         ** Please attach current Dun and Bradstreet report. **

Quality:

Are you ISO Certified? ________________ Are you QS 9000? ________________

Are you utilizing SPC? ________________ Do you have a quality manual? __________

Warranty Return Information

Who is the company contact for warranty returns: ________________________

Address: _________________________________

City: ____________ State: ____________ Zip: ____________

Phone: ____________ Fax: ____________

Parent Company Name: _________________________________

Address: _________________________________

City: ____________ State: ____________ Zip: ____________

Phone: ____________ Fax: ____________

Supplier / Commodity History

Commodity: __Fasteners__   Checklist Number: __2__

Commodity Used On or Primarily For: __All Units__

Length of buying relationship with this supplier: __15__ (years)

Are the quotations from other sources included on spreadsheets? __Yes__

Current Programs

Rebate: __No rebate program__

Freight: __We pay freight__

Terms/Discount: __No discounts__

Lead Time: __30 days__

Stocking Program: __Breadman program__

Purchase/Prices Relative to Commodity

Annual $ Spent	Price Changes in %	Year
$100,000	0%	1996
$150,000	0%	1997
$200,000	Increase 2%	1998
$250,000	Increase 3%	1999
$300,000 est.	Need Decrease	2000

Commodity Information

	Percentage of Commodity Cost	Percentage of Change From 1 Year		
		Last Year	% of Change	Opportunity
Material:	60%	60%	0	Yes
Labor:	20%	15%	Increase 5%	Yes
Overhead:	10%	7%	Increase 3%	Yes
SG&A:	5%	10%	Decrease 5%	No
Profit Margin:	5%	5%	Same	Yes

Supplier / Commodity History   Agreement Number: _____________

Commodity: _________________ Checklist Number: ___________

Commodity Used On or Primarily For: _______________

Length of buying relationship with this supplier: ________________ (years)

Are the quotations from other sources included on spreadsheets?   Yes   No

Current Programs

Rebate: ____

Freight: ____

Terms/Discount: ____

Lead Time: ____

Stocking Program: ____

Purchase/Prices Relative to Commodity

Annual $ Spent	Price Changes in %	Year

Commodity Information

	Percentage of Commodity Cost	Percentage of Change From 1 Year		
		Last Year	% of Change	Opportunity
Material:				
Labor:				
Overhead:				
SG&A:				
Profit Margin:				

Figure 2.2. Supplier profile

CHAPTER 3

Goals and Objectives

Figure 3.1.

After you have gathered all the intelligence you need, you can now begin formulating a plan for your negotiation. It's important that everyone who reads this book realizes that in an ideal situation, everyone involved in the negotiation wins or at least feels that they have won. The reason for this statement is that we all have to work with each other once the negotiations are complete. You do not want any hard feelings after your negotiation. A good negotiator will meet his or her goals and objectives and will also make the other side feel that they have won.

In today's world many purchasing departments are measured by how much money they can save the company. Senior management is looking for a way to know exactly how much materials cost and to know that we are constantly looking at ways to reduce those costs. Suppliers are also working on their own cost reductions. There isn't a single company today that isn't focused on reducing costs. All companies should be looking at improving the bottom line. After you have gathered all of your intelligence you should be able to form some type of goal or objective. In Chester Karrass's book *Give and Take,* he states that "in negotiations, people who set a higher target and commit themselves to it will do better than those willing to settle for less."[1]

So what is your overall objective for this negotiation? All companies should be striving for long-term agreements and decreasing costs for each year of the agreement. An example of this goal would be a 3-year contract with decreasing costs of 4% in year 1, 3% in year 2, and 2% in year 3. Many companies like long-term agreements. Why do they like them? A long-term agreement guarantees the supplier that they will have this business for several years. They can plan around this contract knowing that they have this business from you. The purchasing company now knows what their costs will be for the next 3 years on this commodity. It's a win–win situation for each company. The next question we need to ask ourselves is what will the supplier look for in regard to the negotiation? Our intelligence report should state this so that we can plan for it in our negotiation. Most suppliers will be looking for a cost increase and a long-term agreement. Almost all suppliers will tell you that costs keep going up but they forget to tell you how they are decreasing or controlling their costs. A supplier I negotiated with told me that they wanted a 5% increase. We began to discuss what was going on in their company. He told me everything I needed to know in order to negotiate a 3% decrease. Their company plant had moved to Mexico and they had purchased over 20 years worth of material for the parts we purchased from them. The key point is that I knew what he wanted and I knew how to defend against it. Extremely critical and important is to figure out what your best alternative is to a negotiated agreement. You need to have some type of backup plan if your negotiations backfire. Do you have an alternate supplier? Do you have time to find another supplier? You should also try to figure out what your supplier's best alternative is to a negotiated agreement. Do they need the business? What would happen to them if you awarded the contract to someone else? Do they know that they are the only supplier on the print? After you figure this out you need to list who your alternative suppliers are and if they can supply you the same product you are currently purchasing. This is extremely important in the negotiation. A supplier needs to know that there is competition for their business. By knowing this, their pricing will become more competitive. All negotiators should have some type of fallback position. What is the absolute minimum you will accept? We will accept a 2-year deal with a 2% cost decrease for each year of the contract. A fallback position gives you some flexibility in the negotiation. Ideally, you should list everything you can possibly think of that would add value to your contract. Examples would be returnable containers, vendor managed inventory, consignment, rebate program, free freight, shorter lead times, engineering support, monthly billing, resourcing potential, terms and discount, free tooling, extended warranties, training, free packaging, free samples, electronic data interchange (EDI), and anything else you could possibly want. We, as buyers, have to ask for the world.

Once you have determined your goals, you can now plan your negotiation. The checklist in Figure 3.2 will help you determine your goals and objectives.

Goals, Strategies, and Objectives

Commodity: _Fasteners_

Supplier: _Highway Fasteners Inc._   Supplier Code: _0007_

Overall Objectives: To reduce costs by 25% and to secure a long-term contract with a rebate clause

Their Objectives: To keep our business

Our BATNA: Switch to another supplier

Their BATNA: Allow us to leave

Alternate Suppliers: 1) Hyper Fasteners

2) Nuts & Bolts

3) Fitzgerald's Fasteners

4)

Negotiating with: _Jim Gajewski_ Personality: _Likable, easy-going, quick-witted_

Strategy/power/authority that he/she uses: _No authority goes back to boss for all decisions_

We are looking to get the following checked items from this negotiation:

X Long-term agreement	_ Tooling	_ Vendor-managed inventories	_ Samples
X Cost reduction	_ Monthly billing	_ Consignments	_ Shorter lead times
_ Returnable	_ Training	_ Packaging	_ Resourcing potential
_ EDI	_ Engineering support	_ Cost avoidance	_ Warranty
X Rebate program	_ Terms/discounts	_ Freight F.O.B. destination	_
_	_	_	_

Our Negotiation Tactic: Bring in competition; request that they source from China

Fallback Position: Move business to another company

Trends: Fasteners are being made in China; prices are dropping dramatically

Recommendations: Should be able to get what we want

Agreement Number: _Fas – 01/20/00-1_

Figure 3.2. Goals, strategies, and objectives

<table>
<tr><td colspan="4">

Goals, Strategies, and Objectives

Commodity: _______________________________

Supplier: _________________ Supplier Code: _______________________

Overall Objectives: ____

Their Objectives: ____

Our BATNA: ____

Their BATNA: ____

Alternate Suppliers:　1) ____

　　　　　　　　　　2) ____

　　　　　　　　　　3) ____

　　　　　　　　　　4) ____

Negotiating with: _________________ Personality: ___________________

Strategy/power/authority that he/she uses: _________________________

We are looking to get the following checked items from this negotiation:

</td></tr>
</table>

_ Long-term agreement	_ Tooling	_ Vendor-managed inventories	_ Samples
_ Cost reduction	_ Monthly billing	_ Consignments	_ Shorter lead times
_ Returnable	_ Training	_ Packaging	_ Resourcing potential
_ EDI	_ Engineering support	_ Cost avoidance	_ Warranty
_ Rebate program	_ Terms/discounts	_ Freight F.O.B. destination	_
_	_	_	_

Our Negotiation Tactic: ____

Fallback Position: ____

Trends: ____

Recommendations: ____

　　　　　　　　　　　　　　Agreement Number: ___________________

Figure 3.2. Goals, strategies, and objectives (continued)

CHAPTER 4

Negotiations Game

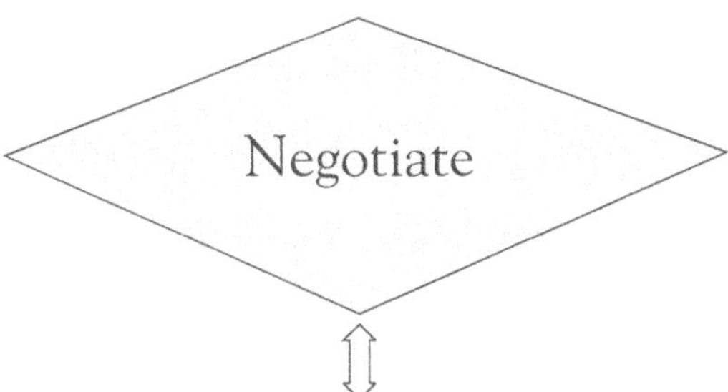

Figure 4.1.

You should start off each negotiation by finding out who your opponent will be in the negotiation. Is he or she hard-nosed sword or easy going? Does he or she dislike or enjoy conflict? How does he or she handle stress and what type of relationship does he or she have with your organization? Sometimes your own organization can be your worst enemy. What I mean by this is that a salesperson may be able to access information that you do not want him or her to have (i.e., the secretary who tells everyone everything). In Chester Karrass's book *Effective Negotiating*, he states that "the less your opponent knows about you the better. You and your organization are better off being secretive about your motives, power limits and time pressures."[1]

Sometimes you need to talk to your organization about the theory that "loose lips sink ships." (This slogan was used by the United States during World War II.) Loose lips can be very damaging in a negotiation. You should start your negotiation by sending your supplier "the letter." The letter should ask for everything in the world as part of your next contract. Why should you ask for everything and what is everything? There's an old saying: "You won't get what you don't ask for." What this means is that your supplier may be perfectly willing to give something for which you never asked. List everything you can possibly think of in regard to what you would want from your supplier. In your letter, ask them to help you reach your business plan. Ask them to respond within a certain time frame to your request (usually 30 days). Remember, everything is negotiable! Once you have received a response from your supplier, the real negotiation begins. There are usually three responses to the letter.

The Agreement Response

This is the best response you could ever get! The supplier responds by saying that he or she agrees with all your requests and is looking forward to signing a contract. This has only happened to me once and it was because the supplier knew that there was competition on this commodity and that the competitors would also agree to our requests. It's an easy negotiation and you look like a hero without breaking a sweat.

The Disagree/Agree Response

This is when the supplier acquiesces on some of your requests and asks for some of his own. This is when the real negotiations start, so it's important to rank your wants. There may be certain things that you don't really need. These are what we call "red herrings." We will talk about this later on in this book. When you receive this response you need to set up a date to start negotiations.

The Price Increase Response

This is the worst response you can get. If a supplier is threatening you with a price increase, you need to *resist*, *defer*, and *decrease*. This is a motto I live by. The first thing you do is resist any proposed increase. Justify it by saying at this time our budget doesn't allow us to accept a price increase (this is a true statement) and that you are under strict senior management direction to decrease costs per your business plan. Defer it for several more months by stating that you can look at a possible price increase in several months. Also request a detailed breakdown of the price increase. During this time period market test their product. It may warrant a price increase or you may find a price decrease. Hence the motto "resist, defer, and decrease." If you have to agree to a price increase get something for it. Give the supplier the increase but have him extend the contract to another year, especially if it's a sole source situation.

Face-to-Face Negotiation

Sooner or later you will have to negotiate face to face with your supplier. It's important to make sure that you understand that only 10% of your time should be spent negotiating while the other 90% should be spent on preparing for the negotiation. Right before the negotiation, you want to be sure that you refresh your mind on your goals and objectives. You may want to do some role-playing in regard to the negotiation. There are several techniques and strategies that you need to be aware of in negotiations.

Buying the Business

Many of us have run into this situation where we have a supplier come in and buy the business by undercutting his competition substantially. Now, if it's a commodity such as cardboard or paper, you may want to let him buy the business. You can easily switch back and forth between suppliers once they try to raise their prices. This, in essence, is a gift to your organization. A commodity such as cardboard or paper is something for which we should be searching in order to get the best price.

Sole Source Exclusivity (Jacking Up the Price)

This is one of the hardest negotiations you will ever encounter. When a company knows that they are the only supplier of a particular product, there is not a lot of room for negotiations. The only hope you have is to minimize the cost increase. There are several ways you can do this. The first way is to try to leverage something against their position. Maybe you can resource some other business to them or dangle a carrot of potential new business. This situation happened to me once. We had a supplier who knew that he was the sole source. They were supplying some "old" technology parts to us. They knew we had tried but failed miserably to resource these parts before. At the start of our negotiations, they proposed a huge price increase. Needless to say, I was despondent over the situation. This company had us over the proverbial barrel. I stated that we were looking for a price reduction and a long-term agreement (you should always try to get your demands in first). As we began to talk I asked about any new technology they may be working on. They had stated that they were working with our engineering department (unbeknownst to me) on a new part for a new product we were developing. All the lights went on in my head. I asked that we each contemplate what the other side was looking for and set up another meeting in 2 weeks. As soon as they left, I immediately called our engineering department and talked to the engineer working on the supplier's parts. I asked him if he was looking at any other suppliers and what was the potential dollar amount we would be purchasing. The engineer had told me that this part could potentially add up to a $100,000 worth of business. He and the supplier had met several times and he was very happy with their product. He was recommending that we purchase these parts from this supplier. The supplier was coming in to visit him the next day. What a perfect situation! I explained to the engineer that we were currently negotiating with that supplier and that they were looking for a huge increase. I had told the engineer to tell the supplier that all testing on their new product was on hold and that we were looking at several other alternatives (we were, but our engineer disliked all of them). The next day I received a call from our supplier asking if we could meet sooner. I agreed and we met the next day. He gave me a proposal for a cost reduction. Thankfully, the situation worked out. In most of these situations, you will get hit with a cost increase. The key is to minimize the impact and remember to resist, defer, and decrease. If you have to accept a cost increase in a sole source situation, get something out of it such as an extra year at the same price or some type of rebate program to offset the price increase.

I was once in a situation where a company was supplying us a mechanical part. The technology for this part was outdated. The supplier had stated to our buyer that they had to have a 12% increase on these parts in order to make a profit. We had a conference call with their sales manager and general manager. We explained to them a 12% increase was unacceptable and that our sales volume had grown with them in the past 3 years by almost 50%. They explained to us that we were the only customers using this technology and that they couldn't make any money from our sales. We were in a bad position because we could only get this part from this supplier. We had tried to purchase a similar part from other sources but failed. We wanted to use the new technology, but our engineering department didn't have the time for this project.

They had tried in the past to use the new electrical technology but they couldn't get it to work. The supplier's sales manager and the general manager would not budge from their stance, which was 12% or get another supplier. We had done our intelligence on the company and we found that they were putting this division up for sale. We knew that they didn't want to lose our account. I decided that we needed to kick this up another level. I called their president and asked if we could discuss our negotiation. I had stated to her that she was in danger of losing this account (this is another tactic we will talk about later on in this book). This division was for sale and we knew we could not afford to absorb a 12% cost increase. Our business with them increased 50% over 3 years and she was forcing us to move the business to another supplier. The president confessed that this particular business was for sale and that she could not afford to lose us before a sale and decided that she would take over the negotiation. This was a president who oversaw several divisions. She was an extremely bright woman, but she really didn't have the time to negotiate with us (you can outplan someone who is extremely busy).

She told me she would see what she could do and would get back to me. Several days later she called saying they would drop it to 10%. I told her it was unacceptable because I could get the same part at a lower cost where the manufacturing process is more efficient. She knew that I knew this division was about to be sold so she could not afford to lose me. She told me that she would get back to me again. A week later, she was willing to give us a 5% increase and that was the best she could do for us. I told her that this was still unacceptable and that I would like to offer a counterproposal of a 2% cost increase with a rebate of 2% on any new business in addition to 2% net 10/30 terms. She wanted some time to mull it over. She came back to me and told me that the best she could do for us was a 1.5% increase without a rebate program or terms and that she could give us a cost reduction if we moved to the new electrical technology. I asked for some time to think this over. Realizing that our engineering department was having a hard time approving this type of electrical part I began to contemplate how I could get out of this increase. There were 3 months left in the year and I did not want to take an unfavorable hit to standards. Our supplier was honoring our current prices until we completed our negotiation (resist). Each month we were escaping this increase (defer). How could I lower the price on this old technology part? I came up with an idea. We were going to bulk up our inventory levels until we had enough to carry us through the year (we would purchase this at the old price) and then we would offer a counterproposal. We would accept the 1.5% increase and work with this supplier on the new technology with the promise that they would have to submit a proposal on the new parts and work with our engineering department on getting these parts approved (these new parts would save us 10% to 12%). If the parts were not approved by our engineering department, the prices would revert back to the old prices by January 1 and remain at these prices for 2 years or until we approved the new technology. This was all spelled out in our contract (get everything in writing). On January 1, we reverted back to the old prices. This contract was a lot of work, but we came up with a creative way to resist a price increase if you have time to research and plan. Sole source situations are the hardest negotiations you will ever face.

Sleeping Dog

What exactly is a "sleeping dog"? A sleeping dog is a supplier in the industry that produces quality parts at the lowest cost and has never asked for a price increase. These are the suppliers that you want to tiptoe around; hence, the term sleeping dog. Sometimes, when you wake the sleeping dog it will bite. Consequently, the supplier may finally realize that you are due for a price increase. It's really important that new buyers understand what a sleeping dog can do. A new buyer may think they can receive a cost reduction from anyone and that as we all know is not necessarily the case. *Never wake the sleeping dog!* The tactic here is to avoid any conversation on pricing and to keep ordering parts. If a conversation ever centers around pricing, remember: resist, defer, and decrease.

Price Reduction Time!

Isn't competition wonderful? What makes it fun to be a buyer is when you have suppliers competing for your business. Some people have a knack for driving prices down. A friend of mine once termed it as "fire in the belly." These are the buyers who love to shop around and reduce prices. Recently, I was in a situation where one of our contracts had expired. These parts could be purchased anywhere and didn't require that a supplier be on print as long as the supplier used the approved material. The first thing we did was market test this product. We found that we could receive a 7% reduction in price based on our market test. Second, we planned for the negotiation (i.e., plan, supplier intelligence, and goals and objectives). Then we sent the "letter." We were asking for a 9% reduction in price, 2% rebate program each year on all of our purchases, a 3-year contract (the triple crown, decreasing prices each year of a 3-year contract), and several red herrings (i.e., free freight, returnable containers, etc.). We received a counterproposal in the mail from the supplier. They wanted to leverage all our cost savings on our sales volume with no rebate program. We sent another letter rejecting his offer, and we asked that they come in for face-to-face negotiations. When we entered the meeting room one of our buyer's quickly pulled out a brochure from his competitor. Once we began our negotiation they started to tell us that they were feeling pressure from one of their larger customers on cost savings and that the competition was heating up on their product. Once we heard this we knew that there was no way that they could *not* meet our demands. The supplier gave in and we had what we wanted. The most important thing that needs to happen before you enter a negotiation is to know what scenario you are entering into (i.e., buying the business, sole source exclusivity, etc.). Once you have this, then you will be able to develop a plan on what negotiation tactics to use on your supplier.

CHAPTER 5

Negotiation Tactics

Figure 5.1.

Now that we know what our goals and objectives are and the negotiation scenario we are entering into, the real fun begins. Negotiation can be very dynamic. There are so many variables that enter into the actual negotiation process (from how the person looks and acts, if they are having a good day, etc.). It's an interesting thing to observe. The best perspective to have is to follow your game plan and use your toolbox. In a toolbox you have different tools that you use for different applications. We use a hammer to pound in nails and a screwdriver to put in screws. It's difficult to pound in a nail with a screwdriver, right? When we negotiate we need to use the right tool for the right job.

Environment

Always negotiate your agreements at your place of business or a place you have designated. Never negotiate an agreement at your supplier's place of business. Set the time and place for the negotiation. You need to be comfortable in your surroundings. Make sure that you rehearse what you are going to do and say before the start of the negotiation. If you are negotiating with several people, make sure they understand what they can and cannot say. Be hospitable and offer your supplier the opportunity to use your resources (i.e., a phone, separate conference room to caucus, restrooms, etc.). Understand your supplier's timetable. This is critical to understanding how to proceed with the negotiation. If they are looking for a quick time frame they may be more apt to give you everything you want or if they have a long timetable you may want to prepare for a long drawn out negotiation. Never reveal your time frame. Why give your supplier the opportunity to know your time constraints?

People

When you enter a negotiation you need to use certain tactics when negotiating a deal. The key to negotiating is to never take anything personally and to be a good actor. Never concede anything initially; let the other side give something first. There are several tactics that I have used and continue to use in order to meet my goals and objectives.

Win–Win Tactic

This tactic is really in the interest of both parties, and it's especially useful in partnerships. You tell your supplier all of your goals and objectives and they do the same. You both are trying to do the same thing and that is reduce your costs and increase your business with each other. In Alan R. Raedels's book *Value-Focused Supply Management*, he states,

> Another way to reduce costs is to develop long-term agreements with a supplier to obtain better pricing and service over time rather than on a year to year basis. The supplier is able to provide lower prices knowing that any fixed costs associated with the contract can be amortized over a longer period.[1]

In order for this tactic to be used properly, you have to have a great relationship with each other. As buyers, we strive for this relationship. These negotiations are easier and they take into consideration both sides.

Many companies have "evergreen" contracts in which they will do business indefinitely without a contract but still strive to meet each other's needs.

Good Guy–Bad Guy Routine

I have used this routine on several occasions. The good guy–bad guy routine is when you have two people who negotiate a contract with your supplier. This routine is used often by police departments. What they will do is bring a suspect in and question him or her. One of the police officers will be pretty hard-nosed (i.e., the "bad guy"). He or she will demand information from the suspect, threaten to lock the suspect up for many years, and claim he or she knows the suspect is guilty. Usually the suspect doesn't crack in this situation. The "bad cop" will leave the room and the second one (i.e., the "good guy") will take over. This cop will perhaps offer a cup of coffee. Good cops talk as if they were a friend and on the suspect's side. What they are trying to do is get the suspect relaxed enough so that he or she will start to trust them and give them information. This technique can be used in negotiating contracts. Who should be the bad guy and who should be the good guy? Typically, in these situations, the bad guy should be the person who has the least amount of contact with the supplier (usually it's easier for the boss to wear the black hat). The reason for this is that after the negotiations you want to make sure that you possess a "good" business relationship on your resume. This is an especially good tactic to use if your buyer has a good relationship with a supplier. I use this tactic from time to time. In one negotiation a supplier had notified us that they needed a 5% increase to cover their costs. They were not making any money on our account and the rest of the industry had implemented a cost increase on this particular service. Before we entered into this negotiation we had completed our supplier intelligence and came up with our goals and objectives. We had found out that our supplier was not servicing us as well as they could have. We had to get another supplier to service us in certain situations. They were asking us to give them an increase for their mediocre service. We market tested this supplier and found that they were the lowest price supplier in the market and that no one could touch them on price. If you are not getting adequate service then price doesn't really mean anything (see supplier evaluation, later on in this book). When we began our negotiations I quickly took the offensive. I went over their delivery performance and explained how badly they had performed.

Next, I introduced the competition aspect of the negotiation explaining to them that we had several interested parties negotiating for their business. I explained to them that we were looking for a cost decrease and that they needed to give us something in order to keep the business. I listened to what they had to say and I quickly excused myself. My partner stayed with them and smoothed things over for me. He explained our situation and also the fact that he enjoyed doing business with them and that he thought they were a good supplier. He scheduled another meeting in 2 weeks to revisit our requests. Two weeks passed and we had another face-to-face meeting. They started the meeting again requesting 2.5% cost increase (down from 5%). I got up from our negotiations table and asked them to leave and not to come back until they had a cost decrease; I left the room. As you can imagine, they were upset when they got up to leave. My partner apologized to them and saw them to the door. Later that afternoon he called them on the phone and apologized again for our meeting. Again he told them that they were a good supplier and that we were under pressure from our corporate office to reduce prices; he told them that I was seriously considering several bids we had received from their competitors and that they might really lose our business. The following day, I received a call from one of their vice presidents. The supplier had agreed to reduce prices contingent on receiving some of the business they had lost in the past. I was agreeable to that as long as they currently met the service we were receiving now from the other supplier. I proposed that if we moved the business over to them and the service level dropped, I had the right to move the business to whomever we chose. He agreed to that stipulation and we signed a contract. This is a good technique to use in this type of situation. Being able to have a good poker face is extremely important in any negotiation.

Red Herrings

What exactly is a red herring? A red herring is when you give a demand, but it really doesn't mean anything to you. There are several goals in a negotiation that I absolutely need. What I will do is come up with some ancillary wants that would be nice to have but that I really don't need. This is what I call "negotiations fodder." I will concede these issues to my supplier in order to get what I really want. I have used this tactic often, and it works. Never be the first one to concede anything. When your supplier makes a concession, offer one of your red herrings. When you offer a red herring, get something in return for it. An example of this would be we are willing to give up free freight on the condition that you give us our 10% cost reduction.

Time Out or Kick It Up!

What happens if your supplier has the upper hand on you? They have some extremely valid points and they are bringing up information you did not know about (i.e., sudden material price increases, delivery and ordering issues, etc.). They are giving you the full-court press and are demanding resolution to your negotiation. They are trying to close the deal. Never let yourself get pressured into signing anything. If your supplier has an advantage over you, ask for some time to evaluate the situation. Try to delay the negotiation so that you can verify this information and come up with a counteroffensive. If you need more time, kick the negotiation upstairs. Tell your supplier that you are not in a position of authority to sign this contract and that your boss has final approval on all contracts. This will give you some time to reevaluate your situation. If worse comes to worse invite your boss to be part of the negotiation. *Warning*: If your boss is not an experienced negotiator, do not invite him or her to your negotiations session!

The reason for this is that any time you introduce another variable into the negotiation, the less control you have over a situation. In Fisher and Ury's book *Getting to Yes*, they state that "letting someone play a key role in a joint decision is a well established procedure with almost infinite variations."[2] If you are an inexperienced negotiator, you will give in and lose your advantage. In most negotiations, you are in control because you hold the money.

Pushing the Envelope

Pushing the envelope is a tried-and-true practice that I have had an opportunity to use. Experienced negotiators know how to use this tactic extremely well. It's a tactic in which you are very close to an agreement with your supplier but every time you are about to close the deal you ask for a little more. One supplier I was working with was a master at this game. Every time we were about to close the deal he would ask for another stipulation to the contract. The way you handle this is by stating that negotiations are over and that if this agreement is not signed as stated you may need to market test this commodity again. This is a firm statement but one that needs to be made or your negotiations will never be over with this supplier. This tactic can be very beneficial if you have a supplier who is overly dependent on your business. Push for as many perks as you can but realize that your supplier needs to make money in order to stay in business and to supply you product.

Defending Against a Price Increase

Sometimes, in our negotiations career, we will be faced with a cost increase demand. Negotiation is like a boxing match. You and your supplier are in a ring. Your goal as a boxer is to win the fight. As a boxer you have trained, studied your opponent, and you know what tactics to use in order to win. You are ready to start the match and win! What do you do if all of a sudden you are getting pummeled by your opponent? You are on the verge of losing this match! Your supplier has made you believe that they are entitled to a cost increase. There are actually three things you can do in this situation. The first is to throw in the towel. You are getting so beat up that you will eventually have to give into your supplier's demands. Your boss may see that you are overmatched at this time and he or she may want to save you for another negotiation. This means your supplier has won. The second thing you can do is get off the ropes and dance around the ring, avoiding your opponents punches until the round is over (remember, you can lose a round and still win the fight). What I mean by this is that your supplier may have some information you don't have or they may have destroyed your argument in resisting a cost increase. Don't be afraid to stop negotiations and to regroup your thoughts and rethink your strategy. This is probably the best course of action. Remember, you control the negotiations, not your supplier. The key here is to research their argument for validity. Use a different approach at your next negotiation. If you are negotiating a highly volatile commodity where prices are constantly rising, try to get some stability in pricing. Maybe your supplier is looking for a 5% cost increase, and unfortunately he's justified in his request. Give him some type of cost increase but ask him to freeze prices for several years. The last option is that you can go toe to toe with your opponent, mustering all the energy you have and slug it out hoping that you will eventually knock down your opponent. You can do this if you see that your strategy has a good chance of winning.

Suppliers often state that, on average, their prices have gone up X amount. Your comeback should be your company is not an average company and that you are probably working on your own cost savings throughout your company. Always request a break down on their increases. Have your supplier furnish you a cost breakdown on their product (i.e., 20% of the costs are in these materials, 40% of the costs are in labor, etc.). This gives you an opportunity to understand their position in addition to coming up with a counterproposal.

Cost Decreases

The best way to receive a cost decrease is to introduce competition into the negotiation. When your present supplier realizes that you are shopping the business around, they usually give you a better price. Never be afraid to ask for a certain price decrease. You should have a better understanding of how much of a price decrease you are looking for after you have done your market testing. The only problem with asking for a price decrease is that you may be leaving something on the table that your supplier may be willing to give you.

Last-Minute Ploys

A sneak attack is when you think you have an agreement with a supplier and they show up to sign a contract. Before you sign the contract they try to change certain agreements. This has happened to me, and the best thing to do is stand your ground. Make sure that the supplier realizes that you were under the impression that you had a verbal agreement and that you are only authorized to sign what you had agreed to verbally. This can be a frustrating situation.

Understand Your Supplier's Tactics

When you start negotiating, understand what tactics your supplier will be using. Negotiation is like a chess match; you need to contemplate your supplier's moves. A supplier will test you by offering a time constraint, delays, changing a verbal agreement in writing, and playing off your sympathies. The key is to understand the tactics they are using and proceed with your game plan.

CHAPTER 6

Analysis

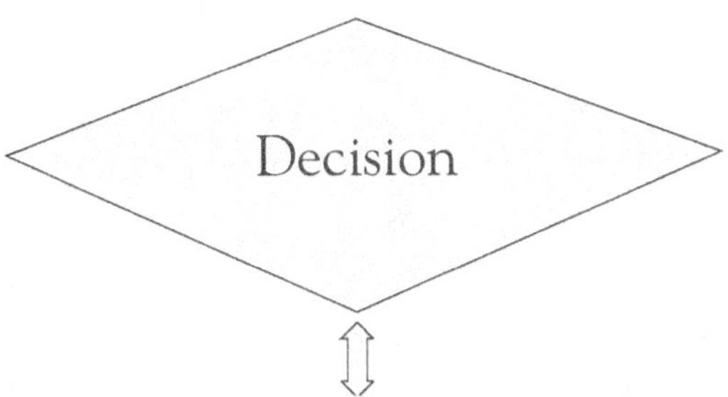

Figure 6.1.

Once we start negotiating with suppliers in a competitive situation, we really need to analyze who we should select. In the past, most buyers would select a supplier based on cost. Today, that is no longer the case. There are many variables that we need to look at when selecting a supplier.

The key point of the selection process is what you are looking for. In J. R. Arnold's book *Introduction to Materials Management*, he states, "Price is not the only factor in making a purchasing decision."[1] Do you desire a supplier that is world class or someone that can give you the lowest price? In some instances you may not need a product that gives you more than what you need. As an old friend used to say to me, "You need a piece of tin to meet your needs versus a piece of gold." Today, most buyers utilize a weighted matrix in determining what supplier to select. A weighted matrix has the things you are looking for (i.e., lowest cost supplier, best quality, best warranty costs, etc.) on the left hand column and a weight associated with that criteria.

You should then grade your suppliers based on this matrix. The supplier with the best score should receive your business. This is a great tool to use in selecting your suppliers. Often we are too busy to actually take the time to evaluate all the suppliers we researched. This is also a great tool in giving your selection credibility. Once we were working with a supplier that we had been doing business with for a long time. Someone in our organization wanted us to look at another supplier. This person felt that another supplier could offer us more options and we could gain more by doing our business with them.

This was a very sticky situation for me and I needed to make sure I understood what this person wanted. I sat down with this person and we came up with what we thought were the most important things for our company. We wrote down these wants, and we weighed them. We looked at each company, and we graded them based on these variables. We came up with an unbiased score. We selected a supplier based on what we needed. We were able to substantiate to upper management why we were making this selection. A supplier matrix is an excellent tool to utilize when selecting suppliers. It removes any bias you may have when selecting a supplier, and it helps you look at the total cost of doing business with a supplier. Table 6.1 is an example of a supplier selection matrix.

Table 6.1. Supplier Selection Matrix

Criterion	Supplier A	Supplier B
Cost—weight 30%		
Risk assessment (financial shape)	7.00	8.00
Global manufacturing capabilities (Mexico & Asia)	10.00	10.00
Transition costs	8.00	8.00
Quote	7.00	10.00
Willingness to purchase assets and inventory	5.00	9.00
Year-over-year productivity improvements	8.00	8.00
Low-cost provider	8.00	10.00
Total	2.27	2.70
Engineering capabilities—weight 30%		
Design services for manufacture	10.00	10.00
Design services for board layout	10.00	10.00
Engineering software (PDM)	10.00	10.00
Technology roadmap	10.00	8.00
Module level	8.00	10.00
Design services for new product development	8.00	10.00
Testing capabilities	10.00	10.00
Board design approach	8.00	10.00
Experience with RF	8.00	9.00
Design standards	8.00	10.00
Functional capabilities	10.00	10.00
Number of mixed lines (through-hole & SMD)	10.00	6.00
Change management process	8.00	8.00
Manufacturing equipment capabilities	10.00	8.00
Engineering metrics	8.00	8.00
Number of engineers	10.00	10.00
Through-hole capabilities	10.00	10.00
Total	2.75	2.77
Quality—weight 20%		
ISO certification/QS-9000	10.00	10.00
Preassessment questionnaire	10.00	10.00
Quality manual	10.00	10.00
Target AQL, target DPMO, & Cpk levels	9.00	9.00
Voice of the customer representative	10.00	10.00

Table 6.1. Supplier Selection Matrix (continued)

Criterion	Supplier A	Supplier B
Quality—weight 20% (*continued*)		
Supplier certification/assessment program	9.50	9.60
Six sigma (Cpk)	9.00	9.00
Total	1.93	1.93
Delivery & service—weight 20%		
Measures delivery performance to customer	10.00	9.00
References from other customers	10.00	10.00
Experience with similar products	10.00	10.00
Measures commitment or request date	8.00	10.00
EDI capable—what system?	10.00	10.00
Knows available capacity per plant	10.00	10.00
Would we be an influential customer	8.00	9.00
Leverage with other Philips Prod.	5.00	9.00
Responsiveness to Philips	8.00	9.00
Interested in long-term relationship	10.00	10.00
Experience with Web-enabled logistic tools	10.00	10.00
Vertical integration (e.g., EE, ME, plastics in house)	9.00	10.00
Easy to manage for Philips	5.00	8.00
Total	1.74	1.91
Total score	8.69	9.31

Scoring process: 1 = worst; 10 = best.

CHAPTER 7

Contracts

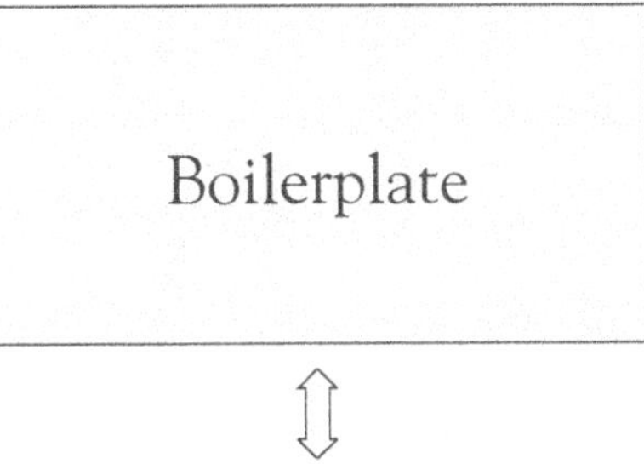

Figure 7.1.

Once you have finished your negotiations, the next thing you need to do is get the agreement in writing. You should write a memorandum of understanding (MOU) right after the negotiation. What is an MOU? It's a memo that states what you agreed to in writing. An MOU is very important because, before the supplier leaves your building, he knows exactly what you agreed to. There are no misunderstandings on what each party agreed to in the negotiation (at the end of the chapter is a sample MOU).

Once you have this you can prepare your contract. Most companies have a standard "boilerplate" contract that their legal department has developed. *Never sign your supplier's agreement.* Only sign your own. The reason why I have made this statement is that your company has invested a lot of time and effort into making sure that your company's assets are protected if something goes astray with the relationship. Your company will have an easier time in court as far as defending the terms and conditions of the contract. If you have to sign your supplier's agreement, make sure your lawyers have gone over the verbiage of the contract and have made the needed corrections. If your company does not have a standard boilerplate contract, many bookstores carry off-the-shelf contracts (but they are not as good as one that would be developed by your company). I leave most of the legal jargon and format to the lawyers and focus on the commercial issues. In all the contracts that I negotiate, I try to include the following:

1. Cost reductions
2. Warranty on material and labor
3. Rebate programs
4. Terms
5. Termination clause
6. Lead-time reductions
7. No guarantees on volume
8. Last-time-buy clauses
9. Price protection
10. Stock rotations
11. Co-op or MDA funds

Cost Reductions

All contracts should have clauses on price decreases, especially if it's a long-term deal. If a supplier wants to sign a long-term agreement with my company, I expect to receive a cost reduction for each year of the contract. How much of a cost reduction should you expect? It depends on what the commodity is, where it's produced, the exclusivity of the product (i.e., sole source situation), and the size of the company you are working with on this contract. In one of my past negotiations, I received a 65% reduction in price over 3 years. You might ask how is that possible? We entered into an agreement on fasteners. We found out through our analysis of the supplier that they were buying all of their fasteners domestically and believed that was what we wanted. The supplier was able to reduce his costs by buying these fasteners overseas (i.e., China). The following are some examples of the cost reduction verbiage I have used.

Example 1

Supplier shall supply product to purchaser at prices that, including their period of validity, are specified. Pricing will be as follows for years 1, 2, and 3:

- Year 1: 18% decrease from 2000 pricing
- Year 2: 27% decrease from 2001 pricing
- Year 3: 20% decrease from 2002 pricing

Example 2

The supplier agrees to an annual decrease in costs of 6% or more. These cost reduction efforts may include process improvements, value analysis, process changes, implementation of enhanced tooling, test or manufacturing equipment, improved subcontract sourcing, and efficiencies associated with the learning curve process. Purchaser agrees to make a good faith effort to review all suggestions for such cost reductions promptly and assist supplier as required to implement cost-reduction plans. Supplier will allow purchaser to review product bills of materials, component costs per bill of materials, labor costs and times, test costs and times, tooling and nonrecurring expenditure (NRE) costs, profit margins and selling, general, and administrative (SG&A) costs and sources where these components are purchased from upon request.

Warranty on Material and Labor

In negotiating the warranty on material and labor, you want to make sure that the warranty you are getting from your supplier is the same or more than the warranty you are giving your customer. If you are giving your customer a 1-year warranty, then make sure your supplier is giving you the same warranty. This is a great way to reduce warranty costs! Many of the contract manufacturers I've worked with are lowering their warranty coverage specifically on material. What they are doing is passing along the warranty of their suppliers to their customers (i.e., what you want to do for your customer). Warranty can be a 3% to 6% cost to your bottom line.

The following is an example of a warranty clause:

This warranty shall expire one (1) year for assemblies and five (5) years for finished units after the date on which such Products (excluding repaired or replacement products furnished pursuant to this warranty) are shipped by Supplier to Purchaser, the date of such shipment being conclusively determined by the date code affixed to the Product, or if unavailable, the date on the Supplier's invoice for such Products.

Rebate Programs

Rebate programs should be included in every contract. If your company's sales start to climb, you can receive extra money for this increased volume. How many of us have had sales go up and the suppliers have received some type of "economies of scale" that we never received? This rebate clause allows you to share in this benefit.

The following is an example of a rebate clause:

Supplier will rebate Purchaser the percent dollar amount stated below when dollar purchases reach the stated threshold levels (see below). On December 15th of each year Supplier will issue a check if a rebate is due.

1% $9 million (rebate check of $90,000)
2% $10 million
3% $11 million
4% $12 million
5% $13 million
6% $14 million
7% $15 million
8% $16 million (rebate check of $1,280,000)

Terms

Net 60 terms or 2% net 10/30, which one is better? It depends what your company needs. Net 60 terms basically means that you have 60 days to pay the invoice. This may be important to your company, especially if you have cash flow issues. On the other hand, 2% net 10/30 means that you will pay the invoice short 2% within 10 days. In the past 3 years, more companies are opting to take later payment terms than discounts for paying early.

The following is an example of a term clause:

> Payment term is net sixty (60) days after receipt and acceptance of Product and invoice.

Termination Clause

All good contracts should have a termination clause. Why do you want a termination clause? Unfortunately, things don't always work out with a supplier. This is your insurance against a supplier that performs badly. The standard time that's used to dissolve a contract is 180 days. Normally, you need that time to find another supplier and qualify their parts. The following is an example of a termination clause:

> Purchaser may cancel this Agreement, without penalty or liability whatsoever, at any time during its term, provided the Supplier receives written notice of 180 days prior to the effective date of termination.

Lead-Time Reductions

Lead-time equals inventory. If you can reduce the lead time, you can reduce the inventory. It never fails to amaze me how little time companies spend on lead-time reductions. In your contract you should stipulate a year-over-year reduction in lead time.

The following is an example of a lead-time reduction clause:

Lead time for the products is 4 weeks. Supplier will reduce lead times 10% for each year of the contract.

No Guarantees on Volume

Never, ever guarantee volume in your contracts. This is a terrible thing to do, especially if you are having a bad sales year. When you put a clause like this in your contract, inevitably, you will have excess inventory.

Last-Time-Buy Clause

Another clause you may want to add to your contract is a last-time-buy clause. Having spent some time in the aftermarket business, we have had to incur huge increases on parts that were out of production. Insist that your supplier notifies you when a part is about to go out of production, and make sure that you are able to have a last time buy at production prices.

What's great about this is that the onus of notifying you about a cost increase is on your supplier and not you and that you have an opportunity to buy these parts at the old price. The following is an example of a last-time-buy clause:

> Upon discontinuation of production product by Purchaser, Seller will allow Purchaser a "last time buy" at the then existing contract/ exhibit pricing on any parts moving out of production. Purchaser shall have 60 days to place a final production order.

Price Protection

Price protection is used in many deflationary and constrained industries (e.g., computers). What this clause does for your company is protect you against price increases due to constrainment and price drops that may devalue your inventory. The following is an example of a price protection clause:

> a. Price Increases—Prior to the effective date of a price increase, Buyer may order products of a quantity not exceeding 200% of the average monthly quantity of such Products ordered during the consecutive 12-month period immediately prior to the date such

price increase is announced for delivery within 30 days thereafter at the prior (i.e., lower) price.

b. Price Decreases—In the event Supplier decreases the price of any product, Buyer will receive a credit equal to the difference between the price paid for the Product by Buyer and the new decreased price for the product multiplied by the quantity of such product in Buyer's inventory and product that is in transit on the date of the announcement of the decrease. Buyer will submit to Supplier within 30 days following the date of the decrease, a list of products upon which such credit is due, and documents substantiating the dates of receipt thereof by Buyer.

Stock Rotation

Stock rotation is a nice clause to have in a contract because it allows you an avenue to get rid of slow moving inventory. The following is an example of a stock rotation clause:

Monthly Rotation. Every month, Buyer may return Standard Products in salable condition, for credit, a quantity of Products the value of which will not exceed 20% of the amount invoiced to Buyer for all products purchased by Buyer during the previous month.

Co-op or MDA Funds

Many companies will give you money to market their product. The following is an example of a co-op clause:

$3,000 advertising co-op fund per model launch

Ideally, you should have a signed contract before you start business; unfortunately, that's not always the way of the world. If a contract gets hung up in a supplier's legal department, make sure that you have an agreement with your supplier that the pricing be in place, especially if it's pricing favorable to your company. If it's a cost increase, you might be able to use it as a deferring tactic in order to save your company some money.

Memorandum of Understanding

This Memorandum of Understanding (MOU) constitutes an agreement of the parties based on the negotiations held on price, lead time, and minimums for the items listed on the attached, dated _____________ (for purchase orders that may result during the contract effectivity period of _____________ through _____________). This is not a commitment to purchase. Purchases are made only by purchase order. This memo sets forth some of the mutually acceptable terms that may be contained in any purchase order.

The resulting Purchase Agreement, if one is awarded, may not include all items listed on the attached sheets. The pricing on the attached sheets is "stand alone" line item pricing. Items will be evaluated and awarded by the buyer based on comparison to other supplier's offers. Those items awarded will be shown in the resulting contract or agreement.

This MOU constitutes the agreement of the parties on the following issues, as stated:

1. Price, lead time, and line-item quantities per the attached spreadsheet.
2. There will be no minimums per delivery date.
3. Payment terms:
4. Additional charges:
5. FOB:
6. Issues/comments:

Buyer: _______________________   Supplier: _______________________

_______________________   _______________________
Signature   Signature

Buyer.: _______________________   Supplier Rep.: _______________________

Title: _______________________   Supplier Rep. Title: _______________________

CHAPTER 8

Supplier File

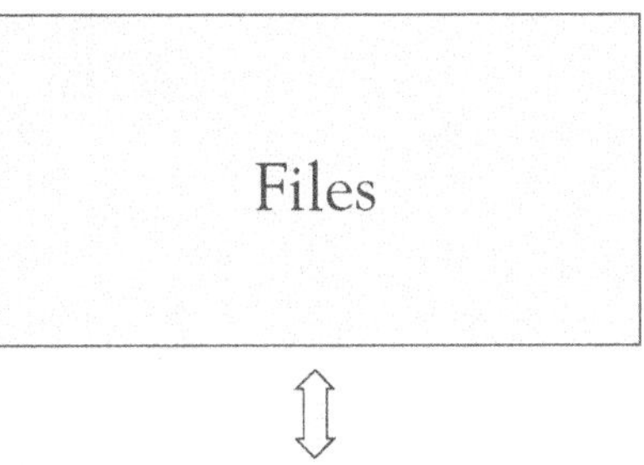

Figure 8.1.

After you have finished your negotiations and the contract has been signed, it's important to keep a good file on the negotiations. A good supplier file will help you in future negotiations. If there were any changes to the standard boilerplate contract, place any correspondence between you and your legal department (showing they approve of the changes) in this file. If you put everything in one file, your next negotiation with that same supplier will be a lot easier. In many companies, record keeping of past negotiations is nonexistent. The problem with nonexistent files is that if a new person were to come on board, you would lose any knowledge gained by his predecessor. We like to call undocumented facts "tribal knowledge." If your company has a high turnover ratio, tribal knowledge could hurt you. A supplier file should also contain all the tools you have with that company, part numbers, drawings, and any other piece of information that may be relevant to your next negotiation. Supplier files are important in planning your next negotiation. The key here is that not only are we looking to control costs with a supplier, but we also are looking for cost decreases.

CHAPTER 9

Conclusion

The End

Figure 9.1.

You not only need a strategy for your negotiations, but you also need one for the supplier's products. We should always try and determine what the future will hold for our suppliers. Michael Porter, in his book *Competitive Strategy*, states,

> From a strategic point of view, it's desirable to purchase from suppliers who will maintain or improve their competitive position in terms of their products and services. This factor insures that the firm will purchase inputs of adequate or superior quality/cost to insure its own competitiveness.[1]

It's important to realize that many organizations are trying to accomplish a great deal of work with limited resources. In this book we have developed a structured approach that can be used in all negotiations. This will save a purchasing department time in addition to building that needed history about a supplier's past negotiations. Strategic negotiations planning will give your organization an opportunity to save time and money during the negotiations process. Once you use the process in this book, your future negotiations will get easier. In order to improve and succeed, it is imperative that you practice and utilize strategic negotiations planning.

Notes

Chapter 1

1 Killen and Kamauff (1995), p. 11.

Chapter 2

1. Tincher and Sheldon (1995), p. 17.

Chapter 3

1. Karrass (1993), p. 4.

Chapter 4

1. Karrass (1993), p. 26.

Chapter 5

1. Raedels (1995), p. 115.
2. Fisher and Ury (1991), p. 87.

Chapter 6

1. Arnold (1996), p. 181.

Chapter 9

1. Porter (1980), p. 123.

Selected References

Arnold, J. R. T. (1996). *Introduction to materials management*. Upper Saddle River, NJ: Prentice Hall.

Fisher, R., & Ury, W. (1991). *Getting to yes*. New York: Penguin Books.

Karrass, C. (1993). *Give and take*. New York: HarperCollins.

Killen, K. H., & Kamauff, J. W. (1995). *Managing purchasing*. Tempe, AZ: Irwin.

Porter, M. (1980). *Competitive strategy*. New York: Free Press.

Raedels, A. R. (1995). *Value-focused supply management*. New York: Irwin.

Tincher, M. G., & Sheldon, H. D. (1995). *The road to class: A manufacturing resource planning (MRP II)*. Chicago: Buker.

Index

Note: The *f* and *t* following page numbers refers to figures and tables, respectively.

O

objectives and goals, 19–21

P

people in negotiation tactics, 32

planning, 3–9; agreements, 8*f*–9*f*; contract execution flowchart, 7*f*

Porter, Michael, 53

price: increase defense negotiation tactic, 36–37; increase response negotiation, 24–25; protection contracts, 48–49; reduction negotiation, 29

pushing the envelope negotiation tactic, 35–36

R

Raedels, Alan R., 32

rebate programs, 46

red herring negotiation tactic, 34–35

request for quote (RFQ), 13

response negotiation agreement, 24

Road to Class A Manufacturing Resource Planning, The (MRP II) (Tincher and Sheldon), 11

S

Sheldon, H. D., 11

sleeping dog negotiation, 28

sneak attack negotiation tactic, 37

sole source exclusivity negotiation, 25–28

Standard & Poor's Profit Margin by Industry, 13

stock rotation, 49

supplier/commodity history, 16*f*–17*f*

suppliers: file, 51; history and intelligence, 11–17; negotiation, 28; profile, 14*f*–15*f*; selection matrix, 41*t*–42*t*; understanding, 38

T

termination clause, 47

terms, 47

time out negotiation tactic, 35

Tincher, M. G., 11

U

understanding supplier's negotiation tactic, 38

Ury, W., 35

V

Value-Focused Supply Management (Raedels), 32

volume guarantees in contracts, 48

W

Wall Street Journal, The, 12

warranty on materials and labor, 45–46

win-win negotiation tactic, 32

World Wide Web, 12